The Simple Homeschool

Christy Rucker

Cultivate Publishing Co

The Simple Homeschool

Cultivate Publishing Co, 2020

First Edition

Cover Art by Leah Damon

Cover Design by Dan Wayman

Cultivate Publishing Co
Coatesville, PA 19320

ISBN 978-1-7354754-0-0

Hey there, Homeschool Mom,

My friend, this homeschool thing, it's wildly difficult and wildly easy at the same time. How can that be? Here is what I think: Homeschooling is easy because the process *is* quite simple. Take a child, teach them all the major subjects, throw in a few enrichment activities, and you have yourself an education. But it is also difficult because it is an emotional endeavor. We fear; we doubt; we hope. Emotions run the gamut when it comes to homeschooling. Logically, we know what constitutes an education and can move from point A to point B, point B being graduation. But emotionally, we get hung up.

I have all the same hopes and fears you do. I had to do a lot of work, ask a lot of questions, and process a lot of emotions before I began to embrace a simpler path to home education. The simple path works regardless of what homeschool philosophy you have or what curriculum you use. It doesn't matter if you are a classical homeschooler or an unschooler or anywhere in between. It will work for you and will improve your life, I promise. It is a way of home educating that can be tailored to fit your specific home and personality.

In the first chapter of this book, I'll briefly tell you about my own homeschool journey, my own particular neuroses, and our family's specific challenges. I hope this shows you that our homeschool journey has not been all beauty and peace and that it will give me some "street cred" with you. Plus, don't we secretly love to know people's business? Check out the chapter where I give you a day in the life if you do.

After that, I will go through some ideas—both abstract and practical—that will
simplify your homeschool. For some, these ideas may be

completely new. For others, you may think these ideas are just plain common sense. If you fall into this last category, this is me affirming what you already know. I hope this book will encourage you to apply what you already know, maybe in a different way.

This book was purposely kept short and simple. You are busy, whether you have one child or eight. I hope, when you purchased this book, you didn't think, "This is it? It's so small!" I hope you thought, "Oh, I'm so glad there aren't four hundred pages!" I cut out much of the fluff and nonsense because I respect your precious time.

What won't this book do? It won't tell you what curriculum to use or what style of homeschooling is best. I can't make those choices for you; however, these ideas will work for any style or curriculum. I know you've spent hours researching homeschooling. Maybe you are new and are looking for someone to tell you what to use, or maybe you are seasoned and thinking about switching the curriculum again. Again, I cannot help you with your choices. But I hope to help you implement those choices in the easiest and simplest way.

This is the book I wish I had when I first started homeschooling. I think of the angst it would have saved me. And the money. And the time. New homeschooler, I hope these ideas will shed light in your life. Seasoned, tired homeschooler, I hope these ideas will affirm your resolve to continue in greater simplicity.

Sincerely yours,
Christy

How We Started
Chapter 1

We did not start homeschooling because I had grand plans and convictions. We started homeschooling because my oldest son, Cameron, was having panic attacks before school in the beginning of second grade. It was awful. Of course, the law stated that he had to go to school, so for the first month of second grade, I dragged him into school—both of us crying, him hyperventilating. Every day, I turned him over to the school counselor and fled. Can you believe I did that for a whole month? I would rush out of the school, get behind the wheel of my car, and sob. Truly, my heart was broken. Then one day, we had a particularly unhelpful confrontation with the school's principal. The principal saw us coming in, Cameron crying and me dragging, and he told us to come to his office. Cameron sat down, quietly crying, and I stood next to him. The principal asked him why he didn't want to come to school, and Cameron just started crying harder. Then the principal told him that it was the law that he come to school. He tapped the phone and said, "I am going to call the police, and they are going to arrest your mom because you aren't coming to school. Your whole family is going to be mad at you because your mom is in jail."

That was Cameron's last day of school. My other son, Brennon, was in kindergarten that year. He stayed there until Christmas break, and then we didn't send him back in January.

I had no idea what we were doing. I had toyed with the idea of homeschooling when Cameron was an infant. I had even read a book about classical homeschooling. But that was years ago. Now, I purchased that book again and began to somewhat follow it. The school, trying to be helpful, gave me some resources to use. I added those and we had a year that looked very much like "school at home." Cameron, whom we later found out has Asperger's, had a very rough year. Heck, so did I. This homeschooling thing was hard. I shut down. The days were long, and none of us could handle them.

I did some more reading, and then next year we tried a boxed curriculum—a curriculum that used really good books and laid out everything for you. It was open and go. I bought two separate levels, one for Cameron and one for Brennon, and we started up for our second year. This did not solve any of our problems. Yes, the books were amazing, but doing two levels made for the same long days. I also wanted to make sure we covered all the subjects I thought I should in the best way possible. We burnt out halfway through the year. What was I doing wrong?

The next year, I would call my approach more *eclectic*. I pieced our curriculum together from various sources and tried to find the best curriculum for each subject: writing curriculum with lots of fun projects, spelling curriculum with lots of fun games, science curriculum with lots of fun experiments. I was so excited for our year! I made the days intentionally shorter and less intense. We had a better year because we weren't as exhausted and we didn't burn out; however, I found that I couldn't get everything in the curriculum done and this frustrated me. I felt like I had wasted a lot of money—money we really didn't have on one income. There was also a lot of behavior problems with the boys and a lot of "this is stupid." Little did I know, they were craving simplicity, as was I.

Fast forward one more year to our best school year yet, I had relaxed a little by now, and I felt like I was starting to figure things out. We used a boxed curriculum again, to which I applied a bit of Charlotte Mason flavor. I was more flexible. Streamlining and minimizing became my goal. Simplifying. It was an amazing year. Each year going forward, I have more and more tried to follow a simple path to homeschooling, regardless of which philosophy I used or curriculums I bought. And each year has gotten more pleasant and less stressful. And guess what? Learning started to happen at deeper levels. When I started to simplify our homeschool, my boys began to learn better and with more pleasant attitudes, at least most of the time.

Today, I do have grand plans and convictions. I am so thankful that we were forced into homeschooling because it is absolutely the best path for our family. We continue to thrive in our simplicity. It is freeing and effective at the same time. It works for homeschooling gifted children as well as special needs children. Strategies I have discovered to simplify have worked, no matter which curriculum I've tried.

Am I painting the picture of the perfect homeschool? I hope not. Let me tell you what I tend to do when all those doubts and fears start to creep back in: I start dismantling our simplicity and complicating things by adding in extra subjects because I think they are necessary or by planning extra "busy work" because that is what the schools do. This will go on for a month or two before I realize I'm doing it. The boys' attitudes get negative, and I dread our school day again. Then I sit down and once again weed out all the extra fat. Once that is done, we are back on track, and we all sigh with relief.

Quick Fixes
Chapter 2

Let's jump in with some practical things you can do right away to simplify your homeschool. I always love to start with what I can *do* before I move on to the more abstract ideas of how I should *think*. If you implement one of these changes in your homeschool, you will start to feel some of the pressure ease off. Do them all and you are well on your way to simplicity.

Bind Your Time

The first thing I did in our homeschool was to set up a specific time boundary for homeschooling. For me, this meant that no matter what happened, we stopped our lessons at this time. I found that the longer our days were, the more miserable we were. I started watching the clock and wishing time would go faster. I started dreading doing school. In the morning, I would put it off as long as I could. I would make excuses for why we couldn't do school that day, saying I didn't feel well. And this was *Mom* doing this. Can you imagine how my children felt? The time it took us to do our schoolwork felt like torture.

When I decided to set a specific time boundary for homeschooling, things got much better. There are two ways to do this. First, you can choose a set number of hours, based on the grade of your child, and that is how long you are going to do school every day. Say your child is in fifth grade and you decide that three hours is a sweet spot for your family. Once you hit three hours of school you are done, regardless of how much material you cover or how much you think you have left to cover that day. After those three hours, all work stops. You make this a hard and fast rule. You cannot fit in one little grammar lesson. After three hours, you are free. The clock starts ticking on those three hours at the start of your first lesson and keeps going, meaning that no matter how many breaks you take or what pops up, after three hours you are done. The baby needs a diaper change? The clock keeps ticking. Your oldest ends up in tears over a math lesson and ran away to his or her room? The clock keeps ticking. You stop to have a snack after your read aloud? The clock keeps ticking. The dog threw up? The clock keeps ticking. Of course, your time boundary would depend on your child's grade, his or her unique abilities, and your goals.

The second way to implement a time boundary is to set a specific stop time. This is what we do in our home. No matter what time you start, you completely stop at your end time. For us, our end time is noon. I know about how many hours I want to do school every day, so we try to start early enough for me to get in those hours. But if we start later, we still end by noon. No school lessons are done in the afternoon ever. Ever. Honestly, my children are so used to this that if I tried to do school in the afternoon, I would have a massive rebellion on my hands. They do not blink an eye at starting our school day early, but they know noon is the cutoff time. Having this noon cutoff time also gives me a bit of leverage—if I have a very reluctant learner that day, all I have to do is casually mention that we might have to go past noon. I've never had to extend our time though, because immediately he starts putting his nose to the grindstone. Then at noon, the books close, the pencils are put away, and we are free to go about our personal business.

At first, I thought this would stress me out and I would want to rush, cramming in as much as possible. The opposite happened. I had such a sense of amazing freedom. Keep your eye on the long view: You have years and years to educate your child. You do not have to cram everything into this day, week, or year. Please remember that public schools are in session for seven hours a day, but any teacher will tell you a lot of time is wasted. I promise that what takes public school an hour to complete will take you fifteen minutes. Having set boundaries around time in your homeschool will be a relief to you and your children. Try it out for a month and see what I mean.

Loop Around

A second practical way to simplify your homeschool is loop scheduling. If you set time boundaries, you will not have time to do every subject every day. This is where loop scheduling comes into play. But first, what are your priorities as far as what subjects are the most important to you? For our family, we *must* do the following every day: math, writing, read aloud, personal reading (silent sustained reading or SSR), history, and science. These are our high priority subjects. For the remaining subjects and for electives, I set up a loop schedule.

A loop schedule is basically a list of subjects that you will loop through. For example, a loop schedule for electives could contain these subjects:

art
music
physical education
health

You start at the beginning of the list on the loop schedule and teach art on Monday after your high priority lessons. On Tuesday, your high priority lessons ended early, so you go to the next two subjects on your loop schedule and teach music and physical education. On Wednesday, you also finish your high priority lessons early, so you will have time to teach two more electives again. Next on your list is health, and then you loop around to the beginning and teach art again. Thursday is a mess, and you barely finish your high priority subjects. You don't teach any electives. Finally, it's Friday, and you have time to teach one elective, the next subject on your loop schedule—music. On Monday of the next week, you pick up where you left off on your loop schedule with physical education.

The beauty of the loop schedule is that you are consistently hitting the subjects you want to include, but you are doing it without the pressure of trying to fit everything in one day. And you won't miss a subject two weeks in a row because it is scheduled on Fridays and you had appointments for the last two Fridays. Even if something goes wrong one day, you just pick up where you left off on your loop schedule. You are never behind, which is so freeing.

In our homeschool, I have two loop schedules going. One is for the low priority electives mentioned above. The other is for subjects that I consider medium priority: grammar, foreign language, entrepreneurship, etc. Everyone will classify subjects differently and list different subjects. If exercise is important to you, physical education will be a higher priority. I complete our high priority subjects, then I teach from my medium priority loop schedule. If there is time, I then teach from my low priority loop schedule.

Break Up with Traditional Schedules

The third practical suggestion I want to make also has to do with scheduling and may leave you cringing. When I first started homeschooling, I was obsessed with what the public schools were doing. I started our school year when the public schools started and then I followed their school calendar all year long. It was stressful. After a few years, a friend mentioned that her family started their schoolwork on August 1st and stopped at the end of April. I was dumbfounded. It had never even occurred to me that we could have an alternative schedule.

My suggestion is this: have you considered throwing away the traditional schedule completely and doing school year-round? Are you still reading, or did you throw the book down in disgust? Keep reading. Hear me out.

When I heard about homeschool families educating year-round, I was appalled. Appalled probably isn't even a strong enough word. *Overachievers. Are they nuts? Who in the world would want to work harder than they have to? How awful to have to do this year-round and not have my freedom during the summer. I need that summer break to recuperate from pushing myself all school year long. My children would die. We would all hate each other. That would not be sustainable for us.*

Fast forward to the year I adopted that schedule of starting August 1st and ending in late April, now it was only the beginning of July, and I was already hearing those awful words "I'm bored" from my oldest. During May and June, the two months between the end of our school year and July, my oldest son's attitude and behavior had gotten more and more challenging because he "had nothing to do." I was particularly inspired this one day in July when he uttered the words, "I'm bored, what is there to do?" My response was, "If you need something to do, we will start school tomorrow." I was going to teach him a lesson about complaining. So, I followed through, and we started school the next day.

We did school diligently for three weeks then it dawned on me that I felt free, just like I did with the time boundary and the loop schedule. My whole mindset had shifted without me even realizing it. I didn't feel the pressure to get it all done in one day, one week, or even one year. If it was the middle of the summer and we had already gotten in three weeks of work, then I had all the time in the world. I could take it easy, move slowly, and enjoy the process. When things went wrong and a day didn't go as planned, I didn't have to feel bad. I had the rest of the year to make it up. We were already ahead.

I backed off our schedule a little bit and started throwing in some read alouds just for the fun of it. Then, we spent two weeks doing only bare bones schoolwork (the three Rs—reading, writing, and arithmetic), and I allowed the boys to choose what they wanted to learn during the rest of our time boundary that day— unschooler style. I started to feel like school was fun. The boys were not complaining as much as they usually did. We went back to our regular daily schedule after those two weeks, but still that sense of freedom lingered.

Have you ever had a lot of money in the bank, either from a tax return or maybe you saved it up to reach a goal? When you have that money in the bank, you feel a sense of security and freedom. If something comes up, you will be able to handle it because you have that cushion. You could also go out and buy whatever you want right now. That is how I felt when we switched to year-round homeschooling. I had a surplus of days in the bank and didn't feel the pressure to be "economical" with our school time. We were free to do what we wanted, stop and start when we wanted, and do school how we wanted. I didn't need those summers off to recuperate because I wasn't running a marathon anymore, I was taking a leisurely stroll through the park.

This idea of year-round homeschooling was a huge blessing for 2020 in particular. Because of circumstances beyond our control, we were not able to homeschool in January and February. Thankfully, I didn't have to worry because we already had so many days in the "bank." Life can throw us curve balls, and the chances of this happening during your homeschooling years is pretty good. One of my friends also just went through a crisis; her husband had a brain aneurysm. He spent a long time in the hospital, and she was with him. When I reached out to see if there was anything I could do to help, she jokingly said, "Can you homeschool my kids?" You never know what is going to happen, and year-round homeschooling can be an insurance against what may come.

If year-round homeschooling wouldn't work for your family, that is okay. This practical application is not a deal breaker and every family's circumstances are different. You can still read this book, implement other things, and have a simple homeschool. But maybe consider giving it a try one year. Start your school year in the summer with some "light" schooling. We start in July, which is when the school year legally begins for my state. Get some days in the bank and see how it feels. Tuck those days in your back pocket, and if you start to feel worn out, pull them out and stop doing school for a while. If it doesn't work out, then next year you can go back to your regular schedule, taking the summer off. I think you will be pleasantly

surprised though as you start on the path to a simple
homeschool.

Minimize Everything, Even the Books
Chapter 3

I really started strategically simplifying our homeschool when I embraced minimalism as a lifestyle. But you do not have to be a minimalist to apply minimalist practices and to appreciate that following a simple path to homeschooling just makes life easier.

Minimalism isn't just about decluttering your home of objects—try being a minimalist like this *and* a homeschooler, and watch your brain explode. Minimalism is actually about simplifying your life to make it more effective, more intentional, and less stressful. Minimalism is a state of mind, not just the action of minimizing. It is thinking: What is the least amount of something that is satisfying or effective? What is the minimal amount that I need to thrive? Apply these questions to all facets of your life, including your homeschool. And, no, you don't have to donate all your books.

Decluttering *can* be one example of minimalism. It is asking: What is the least number of shoes that is satisfying to me? What is the least amount of kitchen utensils I can own and still be effective? What is the least number of apps that I can have on my phone that serve my purpose? What is the least amount of school supplies that I need to be effective?

Another aspect of minimalism is your thoughts about less tangible things. What is the least number of meetings I need on my calendar to be effective? What is the least amount of time I need to spend on social media to be satisfied? What is the least amount of play dates we need to serve our purpose? Minimalism is not only reducing items in your physical environment but also reducing items in your *time* and *thought* environments too.

In my life, I have thoroughly decluttered my environments, maybe to the extreme. I own three pairs of pants and seven shirts. I do own seven cardigans though, which probably isn't very minimal, but that is what works for me. I have three pairs of shoes, not including my boots for gardening. I have gotten rid of most of my dishes except for what we need for our family—four of everything. I've drastically reduced my social media time to a few minutes in the evening. I've reduced all doctor and dentist appointments to the bare minimum—going from a checkup every three months to once a year. For the boys, I allow them each one outside activity or sport at a time. I've stopped buying books for myself and use the library or my Kindle app. My goal is to own less of everything.

So, what's the point? Why get rid of all my stuff? Why stop buying new stuff? Why reduce input into my mental environment? For me, it is about living a simple and easy life. The more I simplify, the easier my life becomes. The less stressed I am by managing all my stuff—tangible and intangible. I suddenly have more free time and more mental space. I no longer have multiple loads of laundry to fold or a sink full of dishes to do. I no longer spend an hour or two on social media and come away with my mind cluttered full of other people's thoughts. I am no longer juggling schedules and doctor's appointments and playdates.

What did I gain? I read more than I have in years. I spend time learning new skills and taking in the carefully chosen thoughts and ideas of others. Lately I've been finding myself sitting on my couch with my feet curled up under me, drinking a cup of tea. That's it. Just drinking tea and thinking my own thoughts. It's beautiful and refreshing.

Minimizing a Homeschool

So, what does minimalism look like in a homeschool? I have taken the same principles that apply to minimizing my life and have applied them to our homeschool. I've looked at every aspect of our homeschool, from supplies to outside activities, and asked the following questions: What is the least amount that is satisfying? What is the least amount that is effective? What is the least amount that serves my purpose?

I started by looking at what is required of our homeschool by law. If you live in a state that doesn't have a lot of regulations, that will simplify things even more. I, however, live in a highly regulated state. We are required to do school 180 days. We are also required to keep a log of attendance and a book list. There is a long list of subjects that are required, and at the end of the year I need to show samples of work to an evaluator in these subjects. I need to make sure that I am not minimizing so much that I am missing any of these things and breaking the law. For example, I would love to just read history books with my children and discuss them, but I need to show the evaluator that we have done history, so we do a timeline. I probably would not do the timeline if I didn't need to legally show that we've done the work. Staying within the bounds of your state law is important.

From there, I consider what is truly important to me and to my children as far as educational subject matter goes. When I first started homeschooling, I wanted my children to learn everything and do everything: poetry, coding, Shakespeare, dry brush painting, Latin, Spanish. Everything looked like a good idea. I had this picture of my sons graduating from our homeschool having experienced everything and knowing everything. There were two things I didn't consider though.

First, if you aren't interested in something, the chances of you truly learning about that subject matter in any depth is slim. If I am not interested in the Amazon river dolphin, I am not likely to remember the details of its existence. Second, learning doesn't stop when a person turns eighteen and graduates. Learning doesn't even stop once college is completed. We all learn all the time, no matter what age we are. If I don't learn that Monet had eye surgery that influenced his later paintings when I am in seventh grade, I may read his biography when I am thirty-four and discover this fact. If I don't learn to paint when I am in fourth grade, I may take a painting class when I retire at sixty-five. Graduation is not the end of education.

So, I asked myself, what is the least amount that we need to formally learn to be effective? Notice that I used the word *formally* in the last sentence. Like any children with curious minds, my children are learning incredible amounts of things every week without me having to force-feed it to them. What could I minimize that would make way for my children to truly follow their passions?

Will my children still be well-educated if they did not learn how to bake bread while we were reading *Little House on the Prairie*? Is reading poetry three times a week absolutely necessary for a good education? Do my children really need to memorize their multiplication tables when we all carry a phone with a calculator around in our pocket?

Interestingly, I consulted a math specialist about that last question, and her answer was that memorizing the multiplication tables was not important, only that they understand the concept of multiplication. But, for our family, I decided that memorizing the multiplication tables was important because it made future math problems easier to complete. My point for including this question and the subsequent answer is to demonstrate that I applied to everything this question: What is the least amount we need to learn formally to be effective?

I started asking this question within *all* of our subjects. For example, of course, we are going to study history. But when I applied this question within the subject, I was able to simplify it. I looked at our history curriculum and saw some topics that were interesting to me but weren't really essential. For example, one whole chapter in our history book was dedicated to how clothing came to be mass-produced. Before the Civil War, clothing was specially tailored to each individual person—either by a tailor, a dressmaker, or the housewife. Then during the Civil War, uniforms had to be made, and the easiest way to make them was to mass-produce them in certain sizes that would fit a variety of body types. Here we see the beginning of manufactured apparel. Once the manufacturing of clothing was systematized and started being factory-made, prices of clothing dropped, and more people were able to afford better clothing.

So interesting. But is this information necessary to my sons' educations? Would they lose something if they didn't know this information? Will they be better people for knowing it? Or could we simplify our history, reduce our stress, and move along quicker if we left this chapter out?

I even began to look at how we completed our schoolwork. I firmly believe handwriting is important. But it is such a slow way to communicate your thoughts. I think we can all agree that typing is more efficient. To simplify things, I allowed the boys to type a large amount of their schoolwork on the computer. This not only sped up our lessons but also cut down on the number of notebooks we had to have floating around. At the end of the year, I just printed the samples of work I needed for their portfolios.

Another change I made was in how we completed our schoolwork. I changed the order in which we did our work. Originally, trying to create balance, I staggered subjects by location and activity. I thought this would be the best way because it added variety. For example, we would do a read aloud on the couch, and then, thinking a change of scenery was in order, we would move to the table to do our writing. Then we would move back to the couch to read our history. Next, we would take a break and go outside. Then I would bring them back in and have them do their individual reading.

My thought was that by constantly switching where we were and what we were doing, our minds would remain fresh and our interest would continue to be engaged. What really happened though was that attention was lost and had to be regained each time we made a move. The day also felt choppy and longer.

I decided to minimize the amount of moving and changing we did to see if that would help. It did. The less transitions we had, the less minutes we wasted just moving around and settling back in. This easily shaved at least a half hour off our day. It also created a less cluttered and smoother rhythm to our day, making it seem to move faster. I arrange our subjects in as similar groups as possible. We start on the couch with our Bible lesson and we stay there through our read aloud, our history, and our science. I put one book down, announce the next subject, and pick that one up. I give my boys things to do with their hands during this time, not expecting them to just sit perfectly still. My oldest might sprawl on the floor at my feet while my youngest would hang upside down from the chair. I require full attention though, no matter what position they are in or what they are doing with their hands. Occasionally, I will stop and ask a question just to make sure they are engaged. Almost always they are, with a few exceptions.

All this practice at sitting had some added benefits too. First, my boys became exceptional at sitting and paying attention in environments outside of our home. While other children their age were squirmy and distracted at church or at a friend's dinner table, mine would sit perfectly engaged. Second, my youngest son has ADHD, and I saw great strides in his attention span and self-control after we changed to this method of staying at the couch and listening through four subjects. I kept encouraging and praising him. Now, he is able to sit and be engaged longer than my older son. The term *training a child* is an old-fashioned term that has fallen out of use, but I see now that that is exactly what happened. I unknowingly trained my children to sit still and engage for long periods of time, which will benefit them for the rest of their lives.

After our couch subjects, we move to our individual subjects. I group grammar, writing, handwriting, and math together—all subjects that include using a pencil. Having these grouped together is wonderful because my sons don't even have to put their pencils down and find them again. How much time have you wasted in your school day just trying to find the pencil that has fallen to the floor and been carried off by the dog? Lastly, the boys do any individual reading they had.

This rhythm of subjects also works well in another unforeseen way. With the group subjects done first and the individual subjects done last, no one has to wait for the other to be finished to end his own day. When we were intermingling group and individual subjects, one child had to wait for another child to be finished his individual subject before we could move on to the next group subject. When I made the change, it cut down drastically on daily squabbles, impatience, or teasing if someone was having trouble with a concept.

Trim the Curriculum Fat and Going Rogue

Another way I simplify our homeschool is to use a DIY approach. The DIY approach allows us the freedom to move at a comfortable pace—either slower or faster than if we had a structured curriculum—and takes us less time to complete these subjects on a daily basis. There is also a lot less headache for mom—less prep work, less leg work, and less thought work.

In our third year of homeschooling, we used a wonderful living history book. I bought not only the book but also the activity book that went along with it. It was a thick large book full of amazing activities to match with your study of history. There were so many activities and I tried to do them all. Were they fun? They started out that way. Then I began to dread them—gathering the supplies, reading through the activity, explaining the activity to my boys, doing the activity, cleaning up after the activity. It was tiring.

On top of this wonderful history curriculum, we also had a wonderful science curriculum, complete with a special, very thick student workbook and even more activities to complete. Of course, I felt like every page of that workbook needed to be completed, along with the experiments. After all, I bought the science kit for the experiments and had to use it up!

We also used a highly acclaimed writing program. You guessed it right: this writing program contained even more activities. But in this case, they weren't just for enrichment. Each day had an activity to teach the writing process. I remember buying crepe paper and brads and wondering what those items had to do with the writing process. Let me tell you what they had to do with the writing process: nothing. Nothing at all. They were used to make my son's writing into a cute little kite that looked great when I posted it online for all my friends to see.

Please don't hear me wrong: activities are fun. I know they are. But they aren't necessary. At all. Throughout history, brilliant minds were educated without mummifying a chicken in a kitchen or making a pyramid out of sugar cubes. We tend to believe that we *need* these activities or our children will suffer. We think these activities make up a good education. That is just not true.

I now keep all activities for outside of our "school time." I view them as extra and fun. I don't stress out my children or myself trying to fit them all into our school day because I think they won't learn without this "enrichment." Now, we joyfully, and without pressure, make terrariums, paint replicas of the Mona Lisa, and raise butterflies but not during our school time.

Now, for history, I simply read our wonderful history book aloud and my boys will narrate to me what they heard. I may ask questions if the narration isn't as robust as I would like. We have great discussions about some of the foibles of history. We also talk a lot about what we would do if we were in the shoes of the person we are learning about. This takes us a half hour at most. I don't follow a set schedule; I don't check off any boxes; I just pick up where we left off the previous day.

For high school, each boy will be working on his own, but we will follow basically the same model—written narrations and discussions about what is being read. In our state, we have to present samples of work in a portfolio at the end of the year to show that progress is being made. For history, we keep a timeline and I keep a list of books we have read.

For science, I do mostly the same thing as for history. I read aloud from the science book, and then we have narration or I ask questions. I don't let it go over a half hour. We will do experiments, but I chose carefully by asking the following questions: Is this experiment worth doing? Do I have all the supplies we need for it? If not, are the supplies easy and cheap to get? How long will it take? Will it be messy? This doesn't mean that all the questions have to have favorable answers for us to do the experiment, but if I don't like the answer to most of these questions, we will skip that activity. For the required portfolio, I take pictures of the experiments we do and include any diagrams or lab sheets the boys completed for the experiments.

For writing, I ended up creating my own curriculum. Since I used to teach college students how to write, I felt fully capable of creating a stripped down, simplified curriculum for writing. I simply taught my boys the writing process without any gimmicks or special projects. I know that not everyone would be able to create his or her own writing curriculum, but I hope this will inspire you to think about what area you *are* skilled in. Whatever this area is, you don't need to buy a curriculum for that. You are capable of teaching your children on your own.

I am blessed with a son who has Asperger's, and part of his particular personality is that he loathes anything nonessential. He likes things to be as simple and basic as possible. He doesn't see the point in jumping through hoops if he can take a short cut and achieve the same result. He is not lazy, but efficiency is very important to him.

One subject where we continually bumped heads was math. The math program we were using at the time was intense. We spent fifteen to twenty minutes learning a concept then forty-five minutes doing a lot of problems. He was incredibly frustrated doing thirty of the same type of problem after already demonstrating he knew how to do them. Then on top of that thirty, there were another twenty or more review problems from previous lessons. I had to agree with him. Daily review of a new concept is essential, but wouldn't five or ten problems be enough? Did we really have to work problems for forty-five minutes? I began to cross out half the problems, then later we switched to another curriculum that was more streamlined—only twenty problems total, with only three or four problems reviewing each concept. Now math takes thirty minutes or so, and the meltdowns have stopped.

These are just a few ways that I pared down our curriculums to make it a better fit for our family. Setting time boundaries around our homeschool, I had to make changes. We just could not fit it all in, so the time boundary forced me to trim off what wasn't necessary.

You Don't Need a Curriculum

Another tactic I use to minimize our homeschool is to forgo curriculum all together. I'm not talking about creating your own curriculum here, like I did for writing. I'm talking about not using a curriculum at all. What areas you choose to do this in would be fully based on your comfort level. When we did this in our homeschool, we cut out a lot of wasted time and energy.

Remember my son with Asperger's and his need for efficiency? I was challenged to meet this need in him with our curriculum for spelling. The curriculum we used in our second year of homeschooling was highly reviewed—as was everything else I used. It just delighted my heart. There was a list of words for the student to learn each week. Every day, he or she would use this list to do something "fun" like a word search or a crossword puzzle or finding a word that rhymed with the spelling word. I thought this curriculum would provide such a good foundation in spelling. My son, however, hated it. It was "stupid." And he asked why he just couldn't learn the words. This set off a light bulb in my mind. Why couldn't he just learn the words? Was completing crossword puzzles actually adding value to his education? I determined: no, it was not.

The next year, I decided to try an experiment. I didn't buy any curriculum at all for either of my sons for spelling. What I did instead was print off a free spelling list for their individual grade levels that I found online. On Monday, we would go through the list for that week, usually about fifteen words, and I would quiz them to see which they knew and which they didn't. I called this the pretest and assured them that it was perfectly okay if they didn't know any of the words because, after all, the whole point was to learn them. Then starting on Tuesday and going through Thursday, I took the words that they didn't know how to spell from that week's list and had the boys write them out. I started by having them write them ten times each day but found that having them write them only three times each day was equally effective. Again, I was minimizing. What amount of time can they write the words and still learn how to spell them? Then on Friday, we had our spelling test, which they aced every time.

Obviously, they didn't need all the fancy gimmicks that the spelling program provided. The bonus was that I also saved myself twenty dollars per child. Simplifying your homeschool will also save you money; have no doubt about that. We also shaved about half the time off our spelling lessons.

Fast forward a few years, I began doing the same type of simplifying in other areas of our homeschool. I began to ask if I really needed a curriculum for each subject. The boys needed to learn their map and I hopped online to see what kind of cool map curriculums were out there. There were some really fun ones.

Then I read the book *Teaching from Rest: A Homeschooler's Guide to Unshakeable Peace* by Sarah Mackenzie and decided to adopt her method. I printed off free blank maps of the area we were studying, starting with the United States. I gave the boys the blank maps, sent them to the US map we had hanging on our wall, and told them to pick two states and label them on their map. For maximum efficiency, the boys decided to label the map using the abbreviation for each state. The next day, I handed them a new blank map. I then looked at their map from the day before and called out the two states that they picked. They had to label these two states from memory. Once they had correctly labeled the states, I sent them back to the wall map and told them to label one state and one body of water. The next day they would get a fresh blank map. I would use the map they created the day before and call out all the states and bodies of water they had labeled. They would label them all on their new map from memory then head back to the wall map to pick two more states. We continued with this process until their maps were filled and they knew all the states and all the major bodies of water from memory. No curriculum was needed.

We did something similar in our Bible lessons. The boxed curriculum we used provided a schedule and various books for Bible lessons. There were five parts: a devotional meant to be read aloud, a part from the Bible itself meant to be read aloud, a part of the Bible that the boys were to read on their own, a book called a prayer guide that had us praying through and for all the different Native American people groups (we were working on American History that year), and lastly, a verse to memorize that was different from what we had been reading.

The boys enjoyed the Bible reading but were bored through the devotional and prayer guide. Sometimes the devotional had us reading the same story as the Bible reading assignment for that week but in narrative form. My efficient son would complain, "We *just* heard this story a few minutes ago. Why are you reading the same thing?"

After a few months of using this Bible curriculum, it dawned on me: why don't we drop all this extra stuff and just spend time actually reading the Bible? That is exactly what we did and now we all enjoy our Bible lessons so much more. I simply pick a book of the Bible and we begin reading through it. Our memory verse will usually come from whatever chapters we are reading that week. So simple and so easy. I spend a few minutes going over people or places with them, if it is needed. And we discuss the major concepts. So simple.

I think the key mindset that helps me to simplify our homeschool is that I now view the curriculum as a tool to use how *I* want to use it. I am no longer a slave to the curriculum writers' schedules. I am the director of my children's education, and I use the curriculum as a resource, rather than letting it be the boss of our homeschool.

I applied the concept of minimalism to as many aspects of our homeschool as possible. The results were immediate. There was much less pressure on the boys and on me. There was much less frustration from the child who didn't care for "fluff." The burden of homeschooling felt much lighter and easier to manage. I also became more confident as a home educator, not just going with the status quo but learning to tailor my sons' educations to them as individuals. The boys had space to grow and learn in their own ways more than ever before. Our school felt very streamlined and effective. This is why I am highly recommending minimalism to you, if not in the rest of your life, at least in your homeschool.

The Newer Homeschool Mom
Chapter 4

This chapter is for the new homeschool mom or the mom who has only been homeschooling for a few years. If you are a seasoned homeschooler, you probably already know these ideas, but the reminders may be encouraging. You can skim them to make sure and be affirmed in your own thoughts.

Mom, you can do this. You can educate your child. I know it seems overwhelming in the beginning. There are so many different homeschool experts telling you that their way is the right way. <u>So many opinions</u>. So many resources. Truly though, any way is fine. It all works. Or maybe I should say, it all works, truly it does, but it may not be a good fit for your family. It will work but may not feel good to work with. The only way to know this is to jump right in and try out a method or resource.

When you are first starting out in homeschooling, it is so overwhelming, isn't it? The curriculum choices are endless, with new materials being created each year. And guess what? Most of them are amazing. But with limited time and limited children (because you can only use so many resources with each child), you have to narrow down your choices. And that is not a simple task at all. I know I constantly have to fight the urge to see what else is out there. I get so inspired by the different curriculums and think about what it could possibly do for my children—increase their SAT scores, make them math geniuses, train their brain to instantly recall historical facts. It is okay to switch curriculums if your child is struggling. But try not to be distracted by all the options and think the grass will be greener on the other side.

Some Quick Pro Tips

The best thing you can do before you start homeschooling, or if you've been homeschooling for a few years and haven't found your groove, is to learn what your homeschooling style is. Homeschooling styles will vary from person to person. Some different styles you may have heard of are Classical, Traditional, Charlotte Mason, Unschooling, Unit Studies, or Eclectic. I won't go into the details of these styles here because it is easy to look them up online. I would like to recommend one resource though, *102 Top Picks for Homeschool Curriculum* by Cathy Duffy. This wonderful book includes a quiz to help you determine your style. It also makes some recommendations for curriculum in each style. One caveat though—this book is a great starting place, but you are going to want to hop online and see what else is available.

For example, my personal educational style is Charlotte Mason. Cathy Duffy does a great job recommending some of the more common books and curriculum for this style of homeschooling, but it was only when I joined online groups for this style that I found some lesser known resources that were real gems.

There are also websites that offer a free quiz to find your style. Of course, every family is different, and your style may be a mix of two or you may not fit into any of these general categories at all. I have a friend who does Waldorf-style homeschooling, which is usually not accounted for in mainstream homeschooling. But these quizzes are helpful to steer you in the right direction.

Once I determined what my educational style was, our homeschool drastically changed. I threw out ideas of what I thought school should look like and embraced my true style. This relieved a lot of pressure and drastically narrowed down my choices for curriculum to ten instead of thousands.

Try not to spend a lot of money at first. If a curriculum catches your eye, look for it used online. Many homeschool groups or co-ops sell used curriculum. There are also in-person curriculum sales across the country.

Try to start out with a bare-bones minimal approach. If you have a list of twenty readers that you want your child to get through this year, only purchase the first two right now. If there is a history curriculum with a textbook and an activity book, only get the textbook right now. If the science curriculum has an expensive supply kit that complements it, only get science book right now. The same goes for math. You can add anything else later if you find you really need it. The purchase is only a click away and will be at your door in a week. You can even get it in two days, if you think you need it desperately enough.

When choosing curriculum, simplify by teaching more than one child the same subject at the same time. If you can do one science curriculum and one history curriculum with both children, despite what level is being advertised by the company, then you will save a lot of time and money. When I first used a boxed curriculum, I bought two different levels, even though my sons are only two years apart in age. That was a mistake. You have to gauge where your children are at, but I tend to move my younger one up to a higher level, so that he does the same content as his older brother.

Do not be afraid to change what you are doing if it isn't working for your child. The first few years are experimental. You have to find what fits your child. And do not stick with something that is a challenge for you. Don't be afraid to stop what you're doing, even if it is in the middle of the year and try something else. One year we switched math curriculums three times in the first four months, desperately trying to find a good fit. Thankfully, the third one we tried was perfect for my son. If I would not have been willing to switch so much and so frequently, we would still be struggling. Yes, I was stressed about changing so much. I doubted and worried. But I am so thankful that I was brave enough to switch and brave enough to shrug off the financial burden of buying so much curriculum that ended up being wasted. Yes, I did waste money, which is horrible, but I *had* to find the right match for him. He wasn't learning with what we were using.

The picture you have in your head of what homeschool is supposed to be like is not what your homeschool is going to look like. I wish I would have let my perfect picture go sooner. You may be picturing a one-room schoolhouse with diligent little pupils happily grinding away at their sums. You may be picturing your teenager sitting up straight at the kitchen table eagerly logging in to do their calculus course. Whatever you are picturing in your mind, let it go. This is not the reality, even with *your* children. I know you are very motivated to give your children an exceptional education. This is a good attitude, but please be flexible in your ideals. Ideals can be exhausting.

It is much better to tread lightly and just see where you are. Then go from there and see what you can improve. For the first few weeks, maybe only ease in by doing the three Rs—reading, writing, and arithmetic. See how that goes and then add in other subjects one at a time. If you have a high schooler, he or she will need certain credits for graduation, but you can still start with just a few courses the first week, then add in as the weeks go by. Your student will end up finishing each course at a different time, but this is usually the case anyway. It's easy for a teen to fly through a course he or she enjoys while dragging feet in a course not liked. I use this strategy of staggering the start time of subjects every new school year, even now.

Get Your Mind Right—Let Go of Public School

One unique mindset has been really helpful to me: I completely and blissfully ignore the fact that public school exists. I don't care what they are doing there. I don't care what seventh graders are supposed to be learning at what time. I don't care when they start their school year and when they finish. Yes, I do follow the homeschool law for my state. And I do consider what colleges will be looking for in high school. But those two factors give an incredible amount of wiggle room. There is no *behind*. Truly, there isn't. When someone first told me there was no such thing as *behind*, I was shocked. *Of course there is a "behind!"* But since then, I have learned that it really doesn't matter if my child learns his multiplication tables in first grade or fifth grade. It doesn't matter if he was reading before kindergarten or waiting until second grade. It all would even out in middle and high school.

To help me with this mindset, I search for stories online that feature homeschool graduates that have not been traditionally educated who are succeeding in life. Recently I watched a TED Talk given by a woman who was unschooled and is just finishing up her PhD. She said that she spent a year tracking and learning about a lizard that lives in the desert. That was her schoolwork for an entire year. Yet there she was, giving a TED talk, finishing her PhD, and generally thriving. So encouraging.

This is such a hard concept. But think of it this way: if your child is struggling at home with a subject and falls "behind," then imagine what a hard time he or she would be having if in public school. What-skills-should-be-learned-when is really just an arbitrary framework put upon public schools in order to create guidelines for teachers and keep everything cohesive in their curriculum year to year. This does not apply to you. You will have cohesion in your curriculum because you are the curriculum director and can decide what comes next. You don't have thousands of children in your district that need to all know the same thing in fourth grade in order to learn the next thing in fifth grade.

All that means is that you will advance or retreat based on what your individual child needs. Forget that public schools and their criteria even exist. You are doing something different and better with your child, so create a different framework for your school.

Get Your Mind Right—Professional Development

Another useful mindset is what I call *professional development.* I am committed to learning all I can about homeschooling and raising children. I read books; I read articles; I watch videos; I listen to podcasts; I read blogs; I read posts in online groups. I am always learning. I have hardly ever walked away from a resource without some new idea. And that makes me a better home educator and mother.

Also, note that I didn't say I learn all I can about just *homeschooling.* Yes, learning all you can about homeschooling is critical. But I learn all I can about homeschooling and *raising children.* Those two things are

[handwritten margin note: requires constant study ♡ to stay current]

intrinsically linked. That webinar I just attended on positive parenting will help me during our school day when my son is refusing to do his history work. The book I just read on motivating children will help me influence my sons to do their best in their academics. Since you are reading this book, you probably already know the value of professional development. Never stop learning in these areas though, even after you have homeschooled for ten years or even twenty. There is always something new to learn.

Get Your Mind Right—the Long View

A third mindset is what I call the *long view*. Unless you just pulled your child out of his or her junior year of public high school, you have years upon years, days upon days, and hours upon hours to teach your child everything you *think* is needed. Emphasis is on *think* because you don't really know what he or she will need for the future. You do not have to teach everything this month, or even this year. It's okay if you wait until fifth grade to teach cursive. Memorizing multiplication tables does not have to happen in second grade. You have an incredible amount of time to teach everything you should.

Don't believe me? Pull out a calculator. Plug in however many hours a day you plan to homeschool (your time boundary), and then multiply that by how many days a year you plan to homeschool. Next, multiply that by how many years your child has left until graduation. You will probably get a number in the thousands. You therefore have *thousands* of available hours ahead to teach. Thousands. Just for fun, when I did this for myself, I then multiplied by sixty to see how many minutes I had. Hundreds of thousands. Seriously, you have time; you don't have to feel rushed or pressured.

Support and the Unsupportive

It is helpful to find people who are a few years ahead of you on their homeschool journey. Sitting down and chatting with people who are making the same educational choices is refreshing. I've been able to sit with friends who homeschool and talk about my worries or particular troubles in our homeschool, and have them help me through them.

Join a local homeschool group and seek out those who have been doing it for a long time. They will be a wealth of wisdom and knowledge. It would be a bonus if they have the same style as you, but it's okay if they do not. If you cannot find a local group, online groups are a great place.

I want to emphasize online groups again here. You can learn so much from other moms in the homeschool community across the world. I belong to about ten online groups—local, state, national, and international. I belong to groups for my particular homeschool style and for other homeschool styles that I am interested in. For example, I belong to a few Charlotte Mason groups, which is my style, but I also belong to an Unschoolers group because I appreciate unschooling's creativity and flexibility. There are preschool groups, elementary groups, and high school groups. A lot of these groups have thousands of people in them that you can learn from.

These online groups can also offer you support if you have a particular problem you need help with. I've mentioned before my oldest son's struggle in math. He had a terrible time multiplying three-digit numbers. He could never remember to add in the numbers he carried. I turned to an online group, explained the specific problem he was having, and asked if anyone had any advice. One mom in there showed me an alternate way to solve the problem that made it impossible to forget the carried numbers. Within two days, my son learned the method and we were finally able to move on to the next unit. I was so thankful for the practical support I received in that group.

Not everyone will be supportive of you ⠀⠀⠀⠀_A_
homeschooling. You will probably have friends and family who will try to fill your head with doubts. I was lucky enough to only experience this one time with one person. It was a very short conversation about socialization. Every seasoned homeschooler is rolling their eyes right now. Take some time to look up socialization and homeschooling and you will see why. It is the most narrow-minded comment you can get, and you will probably get it. They will also probably question your ability to teach your own child, either now or when he or she is in high school. These comments are also eye-rollers. Most homeschool curriculums, if you use them, do the teaching for you; you do not have to have experience in the subject matter. By high school, many students are doing independent work.

⠀⠀⠀If you are getting these kind of comments, you have a few options. You can be armed and ready with answers to all of the common questions by doing your research online. You can also invite the commenter to research and get back to you with questions. Or you can just shrug the comments off.

⠀⠀⠀The most important point I want to make about the unsupportive people in your life is to beg you to not let their negative comments get into your head. Do not doubt your ability. Look up all the success stories online about homeschooled students. Look up the amazing statistics. And this was all achieved by regular parents just like you. Some of them probably even had less education than you do. We aren't rocket scientists; we are just moms with a passion for developing our children's minds.

Commitment, Consistency, and Defining an Education
Chapter 5

I often look back at how stressed out I was before I learned to simplify. I've mentioned in previous chapters some of the more concrete reasons I was stressed, such as long days and too many extra enrichment activities. But when I take a closer look at the difficult early years of our homeschool path, I see that my stress had a lot to do with my mindset too. I talked a little bit about mindset in the last chapter, but let's get more specific here because mindset is so important. Actually, mindset is everything. It affects all of our actions and decisions. So, can I talk a bit more about mindset here for a few minutes?

Commitment

The first few years, I had trouble with commitment when it came to homeschooling. I would schedule other things during the day like appointments, or a friend would call to see if I wanted to go get coffee. It never seemed like we would get in a full week of school. Then I took a part-time job, which isn't bad in itself, but that job became a higher priority to me than our homeschool and I ended up working close to full-time hours. I started to feel even more pressure around our homeschool because I wasn't giving it the attention it deserved, and it was suffering.

Then I started to simplify, and I changed my mindset. I started to believe that homeschooling *was* my job. It was my number one priority to which everything else outside of our home needed to come second. This led to me looking at our schedule. I burnt out at my job and ended up resigning, which was helpful because now I could focus my full attention on our school.

My first step was to make our school time sacred. Nothing could be scheduled during that time. No doctor or dentist appointments for me or for the boys. Just because we technically could schedule an appointment at any time did not mean that we should. I began telling the receptionists that we were only available in the afternoon. If my friend would call to see if I wanted to meet for coffee, I would tell her it had to be in the afternoon or Saturday. Even fun stuff became off-limits during that time. A group of homeschoolers were going to the park on Tuesday morning? We didn't go. We would meet up together the next week on Tuesday afternoon though.

I know, I know. I can hear the homeschool moms howling from here. I mean, isn't one of the beautiful things about homeschooling the flexibility? Yes, flexibility is a beautiful thing. Being flexible occasionally is okay. But constantly being flexible is not simple and causes stress. You need boundaries in your homeschool life in order to simplify things and be effective.

And while we are talking about simplifying schedules here, don't forget to take a look at your children's outside commitments. Are they involved in too many outside activities at the same time? Can they focus on one activity for this season and then a different activity for next season?

How about your outside commitments? As soon as people hear that we stay at home, they tend to think we have all the time in the world. This means that we get asked to help out in a number of different ways. One mistake I made early on is that I thought because I didn't work for pay, I had to volunteer all the time, so I did. This stressed me and my schedule. Cutting back on volunteer obligations was so freeing. It's not forever; it is just for this season of my life. Someday my children will be grown, and I can volunteer forty hours a week to make up for it, if I want to.

Consistency

Another mindset that had to change for me was in the area of consistency. I had to become more consistent when it came to our homeschooling. Actually, my mindset on consistency came about in a way completely unrelated to homeschooling. It happened when I was thinking about my weight. I wanted to lose weight, and it occurred to me that eating a huge salad once a week then eating my regular way the rest of the week wouldn't get me anywhere. I would never lose weight that way. But if I ate a smaller salad with lunch and dinner *every* day, then I would see results. Same thing with exercise. I could go on one two-hour walk a week but not lose any weight. But, if I went on a smaller walk *every* day, then I would see results. We all know this is true—it is the small actions done consistently that makes it effective.

Then it dawned on me that the same was true for homeschooling. If I wanted to see fruit in my children's education, then we had to be consistent. This meant showing up every school day and doing something, no matter how small. Take, for example, reading. It would be rare for a child to learn to read in one prolonged sitting. But sit with a child for five or ten minutes every day and you will see incredible changes in his or her reading abilities over time.

Where is your child struggling? What area do you feel "behind" in? Are you being consistent there? For us, the answer to that last question was *no*, and it was showing.

Being consistent made our homeschool simpler because we weren't rushing to finish the work at the end, in which case, nothing was truly learned. Taking the work little bite by little bite got us to the end without stress. And children really do learn better this way. Giving them a little bite at the time allows their minds the time to process and remember what they are learning. When we were doing our map work, there was a two-week period when I was not consistent. I would have them do it on Monday, and then maybe Thursday, and then maybe Monday again. On those days, they had trouble remembering what-was-what on the map. When we were consistent though, they remembered every single time, no mistakes.

true or scientifically proven

Have you ever crammed for a test? Do you remember what you learned during that cram session, even if you passed the test? Of course not. I think you probably do remember being stressed about it though. The same thing happened in our homeschool when I wasn't consistent in our learning. Once we got consistent, no one felt overwhelmed by all the work that needed to be done—including me—and real learning was happening.

Consistency not only reduced our stress levels but also caused us all to have better attitudes. This was the best part for me. Because we were only spending a short amount of time on a subject each day, it didn't feel as burdensome to my boys, and they complained a lot less. A lot less. School became something they expected like brushing their teeth, so it was no longer like *pulling* teeth. Now *they* will remind *me* when it is time to do school if I am running a bit behind that morning. Consistency is king.

Defining an Education

The third mindset change that dramatically simplified and improved our homeschool experience had to do with these questions: What counts as school? and What is an education? When I was first starting, my definition of an education was completing all the assignments as they were laid out in the curriculum. Education happened during the day, Monday through Friday. In the evening and on weekends, we had off, and that was our time to pursue our own individual interests, outside of education.

For my boys, these interests were almost entirely limited to electronics. It's the age we live in, unfortunately. YouTube was a favorite, and my oldest loved online strategy games. One day we were reading a book aloud where the character took a trip to Sweden. Cameron interrupted the reading to tell me that Sweden has a lot of mountains. I asked, "Oh really, where did you learn that?" I didn't even realize he knew Sweden was a country, let alone what kind of terrain it had. As I continued to question him, I learned that he not only knew these facts but also could locate Sweden on the map.

Actually, he knew where *most* of the countries were on the world map. I tested him by dragging him over to the world map hanging on the wall. I had him turn his back to the map. I would cover up the name of a country, then he would turn around and tell me which country it was. He even got correct the little countries that I hadn't really ever heard of. He also knew their top leaders, military leaders, types of governments, and terrains. I was blown away.

How had he come by all this knowledge? It was from an online strategy war game that purchased for his birthday for forty dollars. After that day, I started paying closer attention to what my boys were doing outside of school. Of course, I already paid close attention to appropriateness in language and content. But now I started paying attention to the educational value of what they were doing. And there was so much value!

My youngest would spend all day watching YouTube, if I let him. He will become interested in a subject and watch video after video on it. I decided to make a list of the subjects, to see what he was learning. Here is the list from just a few months: gems and crystals, nuclear bombs and energy, magnetism, ocean life, the periodic table, various elements on the periodic table, gear boxes, light and sound waves, and optical illusions. Science is his thing. When we go to do our assigned science work in school, he speeds through because he already knows the answers. Actually, he knows more than the answers and will usually add to our knowledge above and beyond what the book says.

My youngest also likes online games and one popular game in particular. Unbeknownst to me, he had moved on from just playing the game to creating objects for the game and creating games within the game. For this, he taught himself two different coding languages, Lua and C#—all before he was ten years old. Also unbeknownst to me, he began hacking the game and posting up his hacks in a hacker forum to build rapport with the hacker community. He got so good at it that the game added an anti-hack, and he found a hack to get around the anti-hack. When I eventually found this out, we had a long talk and he decided to stick with creating. But can I tell you that I was secretly impressed that he was able to do that? He decided that he also wanted to learn HTML in addition to the two coding languages he already knew and started creating websites from scratch, all before his twelfth birthday. Would you call that an education? I sure did.

These instances made me evaluate my definition of an education. I realized education was not something that just happened during the day, Monday through Friday. The boys were learning all the time outside of school. And it was happening naturally. I began to wonder what changes I could make to our environment that would make it even more educational outside of school time. I did come up with a few ways that were easy for me, as I was trying to balance creating an educational environment with keeping things simple and being a minimalist.

First, I got rid of a lot of our books and replaced them with living books. *Living books* is a term used for books that are rich in language and ideas. They are books that will still be read to your great grandchildren years from now. Goodbye *Diary of a Wimpy Kid* and hello *The Bark of the Bog Owl*. We stopped "shopping" our library because the library mostly stocks trendy books in an attempt to stay current. That is to say, they stock a lot of what some of us in the homeschool world would call twaddle. We still did use our library, but I began to intentionally search out and request specific books. The names of these books I got by scouring "living books lists" and "great book lists" online and getting recommendations from my online homeschool groups that value living books.

Now the books my boys were reading in their spare time were filling their heads with amazing ideas—books with rich language patterns that strengthened their own use of language, without them even knowing it. And for me, reading aloud to them, something I still continue to do, became much more pleasurable. Reading aloud books like *The Magic Treehouse* was deadly boring for me because they didn't have any depth to them. But reading aloud *Charlotte's Web* was such a pleasure. The sentences were beautiful, and I would get swept up in the story, even as an adult. The books began to stick with us, and we would comment or joke about them long after we were finished reading them.

I also started to take a look at the *things* we owned. Yes, the boys had toys, although not too many because I was a minimalist. What could I add to our arsenal that maybe wasn't a toy but could still be used educationally? For our family, the two most used purchases were good art supplies and a microscope.

I ordered a bunch of good quality art supplies and tucked them into a cabinet. I would pull them out occasionally for some art time when the boys were looking for something to do. Sometimes I would tell them what I wanted them to create. I would say I wanted them to make an abstract painting; I would show them some famous ones, so they knew what I was talking about. Or I would say they could only paint with three or four colors and they had to figure out how to mix them to get the color they wanted.

Our other successful purchase was a good microscope. I was fortunate enough to score mine used. I bought it and tucked it away on the shelf for two years. I was discouraged because I thought it would be more of an attraction. I didn't get rid of it though because I thought it may come in handy for high school. Then one day, Brennon decided to pull it out after reading a science book that showed pictures of things under the microscope. I showed him how to use it, and he ran around for months collecting samples of delightful and not-so-delightful things to look at under there.

All of this to say that you have to develop a mindset that school isn't the only place where an education happens. Your children can be constantly learning in the right environment. Start looking at your children's free time activities from an educational point of view. Start asking yourself what objects you can bring into your home to naturally enhance learning. You'll be surprise how much of education takes place in the evenings and on weekends.

Present Over Distracted
Chapter 6

One simple and easy way that I learned to cut my stress during our homeschool time was to practice being present. Notice I said *practice* because this is so tough for me. My brain tends to go in a thousand different directions: to-do lists, ideas about changes I want to make, something I want to watch later on Netflix, dishes that need washed. I know you know what I mean.

After I made a few changes to simplify our homeschool, I still sometimes felt stressed, or maybe *harried* would be a better word. I started to question and look closely at what I was doing during those times. Thankfully, I am naturally introspective, so I quickly realized what the problem was. I wasn't being *present* during our school time. Sometimes I would be running through the list above. The to-do list might even have to do with our schoolwork, but I was focusing on the list rather than what we were doing in that moment. Maybe I was watching the clock too much, anticipating what we had to do next. Sometimes my phone would beep with a notification, drawing my attention, or, occasionally, my mother-in-law would text me and I would respond.

Not being present in the activity we were currently doing was causing me anxiety and stress. It was affecting my children, too, because if I was trying to do something else while homeschooling, I would lose their attention. If I answered a text, they would definitely not wait for me. If they were both reading, I would try to fit in washing a load of laundry. They would then finish reading and have to wait for me to finish starting the laundry.

This is when I realized it again goes back to making school time sacred. This applies not only to things outside of the home but also to things happening in the home. This means being present mentally, not just physically. If it was school time, I began forcing myself to do nothing else but school. What we were working on in that moment got my full attention. I immersed myself in my children and what we were doing.

What did this look like for us in a concrete way? First, I silenced my phone during school time. No notifications, text messages, or phone calls noted until after school was over. I put my phone away and did not check it at all. I was so used to my phone dinging and buzzing that I don't think I realized how much it did until it was silenced. I also didn't realize how much I glanced at my phone to check every ding and buzz—almost a subconscious move to glance at my phone every time it would so much as light up. I have now gone a step further by keeping my phone on silent twenty-four hours a day, seven days a week. It is amazing, but that is a story for another time.

Second, being present meant that I stopped multitasking during school time. I was infamous for trying to be efficient and fit something in during the lulls in my teaching time. While the boys were reading was the perfect time for me to fit in a really quick household chore. But, being present meant that I couldn't fold laundry during our school time anymore or start lunch when our school time was *almost* over. Because I don't do well sitting still, I had to mentally adjust to slowing down and waiting patiently for my children to finish whatever they were working on.

Third, to stay present mentally, I began to fully immerse myself in what we were doing. So much so that I even stopped thinking about what came next in our school day. This meant that, before school started, I wrote down a list of all the subjects we were going to do and in what order. Before that, I knew in my mind roughly what I wanted to accomplish, but I would always be thinking and wondering about what we were going to do next. I was also holding the school to-do list in my head and constantly scouring through the subjects in my mind. Once I had a written list, I was able to fully immerse myself in our current subject. Once that subject was over, I would just glance at my list to what was next and then fully immerse myself in that subject with my children. Also, daydreaming was out. I'm a huge dreamer, so this was an act of discipline for me. When a fancy new thought would pop into my mind, I would picture myself physically tucking it away to contemplate later.

When I stayed present and immersed myself in our school day, amazing things began to happen. First, time flew by. Before I would keep glancing at the clock and wonder why time was crawling. Now, I would glance up and think, where did the day go? Second, when I was more engaged, my boys were more engaged. Maybe they saw that I actually cared about what we were doing and wasn't just trying to check things off a list. Maybe it was because I was modeling to them how we should be as learners. Third and overall, school felt more pleasant and less like drudgery. It wasn't something to hurry up and get done because of the huge personal to-do list constantly running through my mind. It was something to enjoy and savor. Less rushing equaled more enjoyment.

A few years ago, a post went viral on Facebook— an open letter to the mom on her phone at the playground. Do you remember it? The writer was criticizing moms who were on their phones at the playground and not being present while their children were playing. She pointed out that these years go by fast and we should savor every moment and that our children want and need our attention. In response, a mother penned an open letter. She said she understood where the first writer was coming from, but she had been engaging with her children all day. She had heard "Watch this, mom!" hundreds of times that morning alone. Finally, while her children were occupied, she was able to take a mental break—some breathing space.

I can relate to both writers. It is so important for us to be present for our children. So important. But man, do we need some breaks for our mental health. As homeschool moms, we don't send our children off to school and enjoy some adult time without them. My mode of operation is this: First, I take quiet time for myself in the morning. My children know that this time is important to me. They know that I will always welcome them into my space, but sometimes moms need some breathing room. They understand and respect this. Second, after my quiet time, I fully engage myself with them during our school time. They have my full, undivided attention. Maybe that attention is divided between them, but my attention is definitely only on them specifically and nothing else. Then, after school and lunch, I need some more alone time for a short period. Just like in the morning, my children know they are always welcome into my space, but that I function better if I have some breathing room. This is easy for them to do because they know they will have my attention again shortly after. We go through the remainder of our day, and then again, they get my full and undivided attention before bed. After their bedtimes, I get more free time. This is the guilt-free plan that works for us.

I was able to get this type of quiet time from when my children were a young age, although it may have looked a little different than it does now. I got my quiet time in the morning because I woke up before they did. I got my alone time in the afternoon while they were napping. Once they gradually started giving up their naps, we still had down time in the afternoon where they could play quietly in their rooms if they wanted. As they got even older, they would entertain themselves while I took a cup of tea into *my* bedroom.

Being present physically and mentally in the moment is the simplest way to improve your homeschool experience. It cost you nothing, and you have everything to gain. There is a whole movement in the mental health field that encourages those who struggle with anxiety and depression to practice being present, which is also known as mindfulness. What, I think, used to be common practice for our grandparents and great-grandparents when they were raising children, has now become something we have to do intentionally. Our lives move so much faster today, full of so much more distraction.

Practicing mindfulness in your homeschool means looking your child in the eye when you are teaching. See your child as a unique person sitting there. It means noticing the hair fall that certain way across his or her forehead when the head bows over the math work. It means getting caught up in a history book, imagining what it would be like to live during that time, and then talking about that with your children. It means completing the science activity right along with your children, not just with you as the director. There are so many ways to practice mindfulness during your school day; I'm sure you will find ways to be mindful in your homeschool specific to your family.

Simplicity for the Teacher
Chapter 7

So far, we've talked about different methods to simplify your homeschool in ways that affect your children's education. Now, let's talk about ways to simplify your work as a teacher. We put so much pressure on ourselves to be organized. We see others with these perfect organization systems; we are inspired and strive to copy it. Or, we beat ourselves up that we don't have that type of system established yet. I have fallen victim to this and have spent countless amounts of time and energy trying to copy what others were doing or creating systems of my own that were bulky and hardly manageable, which means they were ineffective.

I cringe to look back at the story I'm about to tell you, because I wasted so much time and money on the project. But it was a great lesson learned, so I will share it here. I had watched a video online by a woman who had a crate system that she used for her homeschool. She had one crate; in that crate, each child had his or her own color-coded folders for each week with the work assigned. I was very inspired by her system, but I thought I could take it even further and make it even better. What if I had a crate for each child? Then, instead of having a folder for each week, I could have a folder for each day—180 folders in each crate. So, I went to the store and bought two crates and 360 file folders. I chose to get the colored folders because they were prettier. Then I labeled each folder with the day: "Day 1," "Day 2," "Day 3," etc.

I spent the whole summer—hours upon hours every week—putting the boys' work in those folders for each day. If there was a worksheet to be completed, I would put the worksheet in there. If there was a reading assignment, I would write it on an index card and put that in the folder. If there was an experiment or activity, I would write that on an index card as well. I did this for each and every subject. So, for each of the 180 days, I wrote 180 index cards for individual reading assignments, 180 index cards for science, 180 index cards for history for each child. It was awful. Finally, though, after a whole summer of work, it was done. I was so proud of what I had created. Now *this* was a *system*. We were so organized; I just knew everything was going to go smoothly that year. All of my friends and family were impressed.

Unfortunately, things did not go smoothly. What really happened was that I became a slave to my system. I was so stressed out if we didn't complete the whole folder that I had ambitiously filled up. When we didn't complete a folder, I would take the leftover contents from that day and move them to the next day, increasing our workload for the next day. Then tension continued to build. It didn't take long before the whole system broke down. I was stressed beyond belief by this monster I had created.

Relax and Make It Easy

The anxiety that my organizational system created was ridiculous. Now I have a simpler way, thankfully. I do not plan out the whole year in advance. I take it one week at a time, sometimes one day at a time. If we are reading a novel, I read one chapter, or two if it is a book that we can't put down. Then I simply mark the page and pick up where we left off the next time. If we have to skip a day because someone is sick or we want to do another activity, it is not a problem. I do the same thing for history. I read a chapter in the history book and then mark our spot. The next day, I read the next chapter. I don't plan out what chapters we are going to read for the entire year. For science, I do have a schedule that someone else has created. We stick to it loosely though. If we have been working on science for a while, I call an end to that subject for the day and simply mark where we are on the schedule. I completely ignore the labels of "Day 1," "Day 2," etc. This allows us the flexibility to spend more time on a subject area, if we want to, or less time on those things that do not interest us much.

So how do I ensure that we complete the work or cover enough material in a subject? That goes back to what I said in the previous chapters about consistency, commitment, and year-round homeschooling. First, I make sure we are consistent every day. Every day we do history, every day we do a read aloud, every day we do science, every day we do math, every day we do writing. Okay, almost every day. But the point is, I am consistent. If you are consistent and faithful to do even a small amount of work every day in a subject, you will learn a great deal of information by the end of the year.

This is where commitment comes in to play as well. I commit to doing school every day during our school time, with the exception of days that I plan to have off. Year-round homeschooling also allows me a little breathing room. If it is January and we aren't about halfway through the science book or the list of books I had hoped to read aloud that year, then I know I need to pick up the pace. And the best thing is, I have the time to do it. I don't need to feel the time crunch at the end of the year because we don't really have an end of the year. In our state the official homeschool year legally starts on July 1st and, for recording purposes, ends when you have your evaluation in June. These are the only boundaries I have for myself.

Simple Planning

So, do I plan anything I do? Yes. In the spring, I begin to plan for our next school year. I choose what books or curriculum, if any, we are going to use for each subject. I find or create a list of books that we will read aloud and that the boys will read individually. I think about what we need to do that next year and what I would like to do that may be beneficial. I spend time dreaming about what I want the boys to learn. After I create this plan, I go through and edit it. What am I being unrealistic about? Is reading Shakespeare really necessary for my fifth grader who loves the sciences and technology but does not love the written word? Would it be easier and better to go see a live production when he is a bit older, as the art form was meant to be appreciated? Would Latin be useful to my boys? To evaluate its spot in our homeschool, I spend some time reading articles about the benefits of learning Latin. Once I have my edited list, I purchase my books and curriculum. I do not go through these books and schedule them out for the next year, as I mentioned before, but I will flip through them, so I know what to expect. Plus, I just love books and curriculum so I can't resist a glance through.

Over the summer, I will spend a short amount of time coming up with a rhythm for our school day. I intentionally did not use the word *schedule* here. This is not a schedule but just a general idea of what subjects I want to cover every day, what subjects I want to cover every other day, and what subjects I will loop. I don't put the subjects in any kind of specific order besides group subjects and individual subjects.

During the school year, I scan the studies of the next week or two to see what we will be doing in some subjects. For a new science unit, I look ahead to see what activities and experiments I intend to do and what materials I need to buy for them. This happens about every two to three weeks. At the end of every week, I look ahead to the upcoming week and see if there is anything I need to print or copy. For example, I use an online grammar program, so every week I print off the next three lessons. For science, I only have one set of activity pages, so I make copies. For math, I will print off the next five worksheets because we are committed to doing math every day. All of this preparation takes about twenty minutes on a Friday afternoon. (Remember our school days end at noon.) Once anything I need is bought or printed, it goes into my homeschool bag, and we get to it when we are ready. I am not a slave to a schedule that says a certain worksheet must be completed on Tuesday. If that worksheet isn't done until Friday, that's fine too.

I plan for the future years in the same way I plan for the upcoming year. Occasionally I will see a resource that looks interesting for a future year, so I will add that to a running list of resources I want to look at later. I have two lists—one for the next coming year and one for high school generally. I may also get inspired and think that one of my sons *needs* to learn about a certain subject when they are older. Right now, I am completely convinced that my oldest needs to study diplomacy. I have added that to the in-the-future list and will look up resources for that subject. Eventually, I will pare down and edit this list just as

I do my list for the upcoming year, and diplomacy may not make the cut depending on what his other needs are.

Simple Paperwork

While we are on the subject of organization, I'd also like to touch briefly on the simple system I use to track our homeschool and our paperwork. Every state has different requirements, so make sure you are complying with those laws. One struggle I have always had was the sheer amount of paperwork: worksheets, essays, handwriting, art projects. What do I do with all of this? I've tried a number of different methods, and I've settled on one that is simple enough for my tastes. I keep a box in the house, right now it is in our office, where I will drop any paperwork the boys complete daily. Everything just gets dropped in the box and forgotten about until the end of the year. It is not regularly sorted or organized; it is just a jumbled box full of math worksheets, outlines, science tests, and grammar sheets. I don't even separate by child. I can just hear someone right now: "I have five children, so it will be easier for me to have a box for each child." Will it be easier? Sorting out each child's work will be one more step you will have to add to the end of your day, every day. It is so much simpler to just swoop up all the sheets at the end of the day without looking to see what they are and dumping them in the box. At the end of the year, I will settle in for about forty-five minutes with this box and sort the papers by child and then by subject. I pull out about ten samples of work for each subject per child, showing the best progress from the beginning of the year to the end. These samples go into a portfolio for each child, and the rest get thrown away.

For large art projects or 3D art projects, I take a picture with my phone. We will keep the project around for a few weeks and admire it, and then I will surreptitiously dispose of it. I also take pictures of any experiments we do and any field trips we take. Once a year, usually in May, I will order prints of all these pictures for our portfolio. The purpose of the portfolio is that it needs to be submitted to our evaluator at the end of the year. I would probably keep a portfolio even if it were not required by my state, just in case a question ever arose legally about my children's education.

One last aspect of my simply organized system is what I call "my binder." That's an original name if I've ever heard one. I have had this binder from the very beginning, which means once every few years I do have to spend some time cleaning it out. Let me give you a tour of what is in there right now. The binder is blue, and the front cover has two stickers on it—an apple sticker from an iPhone I bought and a "We Love To Learn" sticker. In the pockets on the inside of the binder's cover, I have a jumble of lists. These include

- a list of required subjects for my state,
- a list of fifteen reasons why we homeschool to look at when I am feeling discouraged,
- a list of curriculum that looks interesting to me,
- a specific list of writing curriculum that I want to look closer at,
- a list of our daily and weekly rhythm that I don't look at much,
- two blank school year calendars that I printed from the *Charlotte Mason Soiree* website,

- a copy of an article that really spoke to me from *The Old Schoolhouse Magazine*,
- and a list tucked away in the back of priorities or goals that I have for my children's future and their education—a write-up of what I want them to get out of this homeschool experience.

The very first page in the binder is another copy of the school year calendar where I track what days we do school. If we do school that day, I simply circle the day. When the month is done, I simply add up the number of days we completed and write it above the month. Behind this is another copy of the school year calendar which is completely filled in with my tentative plan for which days we will be doing school. I take a few minutes to do this every year just so I can make sure that I can fit in everything I want to do.

Behind the next tab is reading log for each child. Here is where I log books they have read themselves and books I have read aloud to them. These are not curriculum specific but assigned reading and reading the boys have done for pleasure. I also keep some blank reading logs behind the ones I'm currently filling out.

The next tab holds lists of books that I am interested in having the boys read. These are books pulled from websites that make recommendations like "50 Great Books" or "10 Classics Every Child Should Read." I also am part some homeschooling groups online that value quality books, and people will occasionally make recommendations there. These go on these lists too.

The last tab is what I consider the legal tab. I have my HSLDA (Home School Legal Defense Association) membership cards here. Then I have copies of all the documents I am required to turn in to my school district by law: an affidavit stating that I will be homeschooling in compliance with the law, a copy of my evaluator's end-of-year form, medical and dental forms that I need to keep on record, and the letter from the school district saying I am in compliance and will be homeschooling for the year. In the very back pocket of the back cover of the binder I have tucked my receipts from sending my legal forms to the school district certified mail with a signature. I also have the signature cards from the mailing that have come back to me to keep as proof that the school district has received my forms.

Looking at what I just wrote about my binder, I see that it looks like a lot and almost looks complicated. Truly though, on a daily basis, I spend a total of one minute in this binder, checking off the day we completed on the calendar or writing down a book my children may have finished reading. The rest just gets stuffed in there and then pulled out when I am planning for the next year. It is truly low-key and simple.

Consuming Homeschool Content
Chapter 8

Great blogs, podcasts, and groups online for and about homeschooling abound. When I first started homeschooling, I spent a lot of time online reading and pinning articles on Pinterest; however, with such an overwhelming amount of information, you are never sure which is right, and much of it is conflicting. Classical homeschooling is rigorous and has a proven track record, as does unschooling, which is very relaxed. It reminds me so much of the diet industry: Are eggs good or bad? Is fat evil or necessary? Carbs or no carbs? The answer depends on who you ask, but they are all experts. So, whom do you believe?

Homeschooling felt like the diet industry to me. Which was right? I wavered back and forth between styles for a long time. I thought for sure the Classical method was going to be the right fit for us. Then I backtracked and tried traditional methods. Then we did Charlotte Mason because that looked like the perfect one. I even flirted with unschooling for a few months. I was getting so much input from the online world that I couldn't make up my mind on what was the *right* way. What I didn't know was there is no right way. Or, I should say, they are all the right way.

When settled on a style, I started consuming online content about that specific style. Even within a specific style, I found conflicting information. I found some really good ideas and some really bad ideas. I found so many ideas that I overwhelmed myself trying to do them all or trying to figure out which conflicting piece of advice was correct.

All homeschooling styles can be effective. However, the vast amount of content online and the varying opinions about differing styles may overwhelm even a veteran homeschooler. I want to encourage you to simplify your homeschool by limiting exposure to this content. Some online content is very good and incredibly helpful. Other online content is not helpful at all. It isn't bad; it just isn't helpful. Let me give you some examples and suggest what to look for.

Online Homeschool Groups—the Good and the Bad

I am in about twelve online groups full of different kinds of homeschoolers. Twelve is actually a lot for me, but some of these groups are very narrow in topic, which means they aren't heavily active. Other groups are for a certain curriculum or for a certain style of homeschooling. I was in one general homeschooling group, but I jumped ship after only a few days because they seemed to talk about everything but homeschooling. If you are just looking to shoot the breeze with other moms that also happen to homeschool, those are great. But I need, and am more interested in, groups that provide real value and support to my homeschool.

The best groups I am in have a very rigorous vetting process for joining and the admins are very active. They will not allow any off-topic posts or questions in posts that a quick search with the search bar could answer. These groups are a gold mine of resources. They are specific to the niche they serve and therefore very helpful. These types are the ones I suggest you join. I however made one personal exception to this: a group that is so positive and encouraging that I love being part of it.

The talk is more general but does stay on the homeschooling topic 90 percent of the time.

One trouble I have found with online groups is that they are the prime spot for conflicting information. They are full of people just like you and me, regular moms and dads, who may not have really gone in depth with a topic. He or she will make a recommendation because a sister's friend's cousin did it that way and it worked for them. Use these groups strategically. My mode of operation is to post in the group with the intent to gather as much specific information as possible then I will do further research to narrow down. For example, I will not post a question that says, "Help! My seventh grader just cannot write a paragraph. What should I do?" This type of questions will get answers that run the gamut from *put him into public school* to *make sure to get his hand x-rayed because he may have a fracture.* We have all had this experience online. What I do instead is ask a question that will give me information to work with for my own research. So, I may ask, "What writing curriculum are you using for your middle schooler who hates writing? Do you like it or hate it? Why?" I then take all of those recommendations, the good and the bad, and do my own research, reading reviews and looking at content. This way I get to see what is out there, things that may not be in the mainstream homeschooling sphere, and I avoid all the flotsam that is part of the online world.

Blogs and Podcasts—the Good and the Bad

I have similar criteria for blogs and podcasts: useful and not useful. Anyone can have a blog today. It is simple and easy to set up. Writing a blog post can take all of fifteen minutes. Having a blog does not make you an expert. I personally avoid the blogs that are more of what I consider "lifestyle." These blogs tell about what they are doing in their homeschool day or what fun field trip they just took. A recipe for their favorite cinnamon buns may be included. To me, these blogs are not useful and a time waster. They may have a few pinnable ideas or craft projects, but are not helpful as far as homeschooling goes. You will recognize these blogs by the plethora of ads, none of which have anything to do with homeschooling, that make it hard to get to the content.

The same goes for podcasts. The ones that aren't useful are usually just talking about the homeschool lifestyle and interview different kinds of homeschoolers. These podcasts are good when you are just starting out but do not offer a lot of in-depth information or ideas. Occasionally I do search these sources out to feel connected and inspired, but I don't let this type of content take up too much of my time. Again, these podcasts aren't bad, but I only have short periods of time to listen and like to choose ones that help me in my homeschool.

Then you have the blogs and podcasts that are especially useful. Many times, these good ones will not have ads or the ads will be targeted specifically for the homeschool community. These blogs and podcasts are full of detailed and precise information—how-to manuals and professional development for the homeschooler based on years of experience and research. You will not likely find any recipes or craft projects. These hard-core homeschoolers are not looking to increase their click rate but are truly looking to serve the homeschool community. These are the outliers.

Printed Media—the Good and the Bad

A few magazines specific to home education are still in print, and I've found that they vary in helpfulness. I look for magazines that contain articles from experts in their field. An expert would be someone who is writing about a subject they have training in: a reading specialist on teaching your child to read, a veterinarian on dissection, or a mathematician on the importance of algebra. Not every article has to be from an expert, but there needs to be some expertise between the pages to warrant using my limited time to read it.

One magazine I found was just gorgeous: no ads (so it was expensive), good quality paper, and beautiful photos. It was very well put together. I eagerly read through it; however, when I came to the end, I didn't really have anything useful to think about or apply. I felt good reading the stories, but it didn't practically serve me or give me any new thoughts to think. I then looked at who the writers were, none were experts in anything. Most were social media influencers or bloggers. Some didn't even have school age children yet. I did really enjoy this magazine, and it did have incredible inspirational value, but again, with limited time, I need to choose my resources wisely.

I don't mind advertising in homeschooling magazines because the ads help keep *my* cost down. The advertisers help pay for the magazine's full cost of production instead of me. And because most ads in homeschool magazines are homeschool-relevant, I see what resources are out there that I might be missing. But most of all, I want to see input from experts and practical advice along with the inspirational articles.

My whole point here is that your time is precious. You are a mom. That automatically makes you busy. You can read all day long, but if you aren't curating what you are reading, you are wasting precious time and energy. Yes, if you had all the time in the world, there may be some small thing that you could learn from all those online groups, blogs, podcasts, and magazines. At the very least, I know you would be encouraged by them. But time is a finite resource, so you need to go to the best of the best.

The Best of the Best

The best of the best, for me, means books. A certain authority comes with a printed book. First, only someone with experience will write a book. Writing a book takes a lot of time and energy. It is hard. The formation of a book is a kind of crucible. Many may start a book, but only those who truly have something to teach others will finish it. Then there is the entire publishing process to get through. Writing a book is not for everyone. You have to want to serve the homeschool community to put the effort into writing a book about homeschooling. You usually won't find yummy recipes and fun crafts in a book that helps you be a better homeschool parent. Books are where you get to the meat of the subject; this is why they are my prime pick for finding information.

After a few years of homeschooling, I started putting these guidelines into practice and stopped bouncing like a ping-pong ball. I only stayed in the homeschool groups online that focused specifically on homeschooling, not on family lifestyle. I started only taking in the best websites and podcasts for homeschooling. And

I started reading magazine articles from experts and published books full of great information. I settled down and was able to focus on what was best for my family, using my own brain to solve problems. And I found other moms and dads who have been through the flames a few times and have the scars to prove it.

Necessities for an Education
Chapter 9

I'm a dreamer and an abstract thinker. I can spend hours fantasizing and elaborating on one imaginary scenario. This is my way of processing questions I have about who I am, who other people are, and what the world is like. I am probably a philosopher. I'm not sure if that is a good quality of mine, or one that isn't worthwhile. It actually may be a time waster.

Here is one question I've spent a lot of time considering and fantasizing about: What do you *truly, actually* need to be educated? This is the question at the core of this whole book. What is essential to the education of a child? What brings value to a child's education? Of course, the answers will be different for each family, even for each child, but there are some answers we can give here.

What is Needed?

I like to think of two different scenarios. First, what if I was in charge of my children's education during the early 1800s? What tools would I have used to educate them? Second, what if there was a major event that fundamentally changed life as we know it now? What if there would be no expectations, no regulations, and no boundaries? What tools would I then use to educate my children? I think the answers for both scenarios are the same.

First, I ask, would my children need an education? I always answer *yes* to this question, which leads me to ask why? What value is education? Could they just simply learn a trade? This is a valuable question to ask, even in real life. Is a person's life improved by having a broad education? Is a doctor a better doctor because he or she read Shakespeare? Is a CEO a better CEO because he or she knows that two hydrogen atoms and one oxygen atom make water?

I've decided that Charlotte Mason was right. A rich education comes down to ideas—learning ideas, evaluating ideas, and creating ideas. Ideas are the feast of thinkers. A person who can think clearly and well will prosper in any field he or she chooses. A doctor is not better at stitching up a patient because he or she knows Shakespeare but because encountering Shakespeare forced thinking, using the brain in a different way. Thinking clearly and well is a skill that needs to be learned, and the path to learning that is by encountering a wide variety of ideas and thoughts.

So, if I were fantasizing about educating during a crisis situation, I know I would need books. A lot of books. I do not mean textbooks, but well-written books by people who are passionate about what they are writing and an expert in the content area. In the beginning, I would need books that are simply written in order to teach reading. As my children get older, I would need books that use more advanced language and contain a wealth of ideas. I would look for well-written fiction and non-fiction. I would also probably skip right to books that are higher level because resources would be scarce. I would forgo books like the Magic Treehouse series and search for Shakespeare and Dickens.

Science would be essential because we have to know how our world works. I may use a well-written textbook for this if I could find it but would more likely hunt for books that deal with one specific topic at a time—cells, weather, mechanical advantage, and so on.

History is equally important. Like science, I would search for quality books that discuss one era, aspect, or person of history at a time. I would look for books on broad topics, such as the Middle Ages, and more specific areas, like the writing of the American Constitution.

Once a person has ideas, he or she needs to be able to articulate them. This means that a medium for writing is needed—pencils and paper. It also means that good books are needed to show us good examples of writing. With these three things—ideas, writing mediums, and good books—a person can go a long way in being educated.

I would also put emphasis on communicating ideas clearly through speech. I would use poetry recitation to start my children on their path to public speaking. Once older, I would work with them on the art of communicating their ideas orally as well as debating a point properly.

Also fundamental to their education would be math. You need math, regardless of how useless your thirteen-year-old says it is. Personally, math is my weakest area, so a basic text is necessary to help me through. I don't need a lot of frills or a lot of explanation, but I do need a resource.

As I would want my children to speak a second language, I would find a person who is bilingual to tutor them one-on-one. This is really the best way to learn a language in any scenario.

Geography would be a priority for us as well. For this, we would need a map or a globe at the minimum. A well-written geography resource would also be ideal.

I love philosophy. I agree with Socrates that "the unexamined life is not worth living." On my wish list of essentials of an education would be books of the great philosophers of history. Again, this comes back to ideas. If you are looking for some ideas to feast on, philosophy is a rich source.

My goal for all these books and resources would be to train my children to be thinkers. To evaluate ideas, they must encounter and form ideas of their own. This is what I believe is the essence of education.

Besides a wide variety of books, the other valuable tool I would use is discussion. To read a fact is to learn a fact, maybe; but to discuss a fact is to then learn the depths of the fact—to learn what that fact truly means.

These are my answers to the philosophical questions about what is really needed for an education. If you are also someone who likes to contemplate questions like this, you may come up with different answers. The point is, we can use our answers to guide how we choose to educate our children today in real life. These questions helps us form ideals for our homeschool that we can then put into practice, simplifying the act of educating our children to what we feel is essential.

Discussion and Learning

This thought bears repeating: To read a fact is to learn a fact, maybe; but to discuss a fact is to learn the *depths* of the fact—to learn what that fact truly means. I'd like to add a bit to the last part of that sentence. I'd like it to say, "to learn what that fact truly means . . . to the person and to the world."

Discussion is the simplest form of education there is. It has been used for millennia to shape young minds. Most of us have heard of the Socratic method, where you ask questions to promote critical thinking and debate. Many upper level college courses use discussion as their backbone. It is such an effective way to learn.

In our homeschool, we cut out the extra fluff and we replace it with discussion. Discussions are great for the homeschool mom because there is zero prep work. You don't have to cut or laminate anything. You don't have to go out and buy the supplies. You don't even need to find the pencils and the notebook that got pushed under the couch. And, best of all, discussion is free.

I usually don't prep discussion questions, although I will glance over the questions in a curriculum to see if there is anything useful there. Most of the time though, I'm just curious about my sons' thoughts on what we read.

For example, for history, I would ask questions like the following: Do you think the people who owned slaves were bad people? Was it okay that they were just going along with the societal norm? What if you were a slave during that time? We are a mixed-race family. My children's ancestors on their father's side were slaves, so I also asked how they felt knowing their great-great-great grandparents were slaves. Did that affect them today? Does that affect how they view themselves?

For science, I've asked questions like the following: What if gravity weren't as heavy, what would change? Would our bone density change? How about our muscle tone? Would there be less ailments like arthritis or fallen arches? (They didn't know what fallen arches were.)

For math, we talk about things like how flat you can make a triangle before it turns into a line. When we work out large multiplication problems, we pretend we are getting that much money in our bank account and talk about what we would do with it.

We are all quiet introverts in our family, except my youngest, so talk doesn't necessarily come easy to us. But if I hit on a good discussion question, things can get lively. I say this, because if you are an introvert and value quiet like we do, I promise you that discussions aren't as painful as they sound.

I never force or push a conversation. If the question isn't a winner, I will ask another question, or we will just move on to the next subject. Forced conversation isn't fun for anyone and would not be a great learning tool.

If you have trouble coming up with questions, the internet is a good resource. You can type in "discussion questions for _____" and find a lot of websites with suggestions. Some questions are bad and others are good, so you will have to use your discernment.

Sometimes, conversations may not go as planned. Children can ask some really hard or uncomfortable questions during discussions. Sometimes my boys would ask things that made me cringe to answer, things I wished their innocent minds wouldn't have even been able to come up with. But I am committed to answering as honestly as I can and as best as I can. Now that they are older, it is easier because I do not have to filter as much. This will be different for every family though.

During discussion times, I don't try to direct the conversation much. I am the facilitator, but I let my boys do most of the talking. If they ask a question, much of the time I will just respond with "What do *you* think?" I will ask questions to push their buttons or challenge them on a thought if I feel it is appropriate. But mostly I just listen. This isn't the time for teaching or imparting facts; it is the time for their young minds to be exploring their own thoughts and conclusions based on the facts they just learned.

A Day in the Life
Chapter 10

Would you like to hear how all of these ideas come together in daily life? What follows is a pretty typical school day for us. I think it shows our flow and our simplicity. There is no rush or hurry, no cracking of the whip. To me, it feels like there is a gentle rhythm. It is an easy day to live, not one that makes me dread facing it.

I will only include the formal school part, not our entire day. For your curiosity, after our school day is done, both boys are allowed on electronics. Brennon, my youngest, gets online and starts writing script to create new items for him and his friends on Roblox. He will spend the next few hours lost in code, while listening to—not watching—one of his few favorite shows on Netflix. Cameron, my eldest, also hits his computer to play intense, hours-long strategy games with people from around the world. The information he knows about other cultures just from playing online with other kids and adults around the world is amazing. I always am surprised when he talks about his friend in Sweden or his friend in Britain. His plan is to start recording segments of these games, editing the videos, and posting them on YouTube.

After reading this, you may also be wondering why I am still reading aloud history and science books to my now middle-school aged children. Reading aloud is so important, even into the teenage years. It builds vocabulary and patterns of speech in their minds in a way that reading to themselves does not. Yes, it would be simpler to just hand them the books. But I feel there is more value in reading aloud to them as much as I can. (Andrew Pudewa has a wonderful talk "Nurturing

Competent Communicators" on YouTube, if you are interested in this idea.)

Our Simple Homeschool Day

I am sitting on the couch, stunned from finding myself awake early in the morning, sipping on a cup of coffee while trying to swim up through the fog. I am stunned every morning when I wake up, the effect of waking up early but not being a morning person. My husband is usually up hours before I am, but he knows not to engage with me too much beyond "good morning." I'm not a grumpy non-morning person; I just don't process well in the morning. You can come and sit down and tell me all about what is on your mind, and I will just stare blankly at you, trying to decode the words you are using. This is why it is essential that I wake up at least an hour before my children. They are not as sensitive to my needs in the morning as my husband is. It's not so bad now that they are older, because they sleep in later. They usually come out of their room around 8:30, so if I wake up at 7:30, I'm safe.

That 8:30 hour is approaching, my coffee is almost finished and I'm starting to feel clearer headed. I hear thumping feet and the boys' bedroom door bangs open. I know it is Brennon. He is least reserved of all of us, even in his movements. Cameron will come out so quietly that you don't even realize he's out until you see him coming down the hall—half lumbering, half swaggering—the way tall, thirteen-year-old boys do. Usually Brennon is first though because an optimistic eleven-year-old isn't interested in laying moodily in bed like his more mature thirteen-year-old brother.

"Good morning," Brennon says as he sits down in *his* chair. We each have our own favorite spot in our living room. After few moments of quiet, he says, "Let's start school." I chuckle because it is still a bit early for my tastes, but he is ready to go.

"OK, I have to wake up Cameron and eat breakfast." Brennon practices intermittent fasting by skipping breakfast every day, unless he decides he is making pancakes for the family. I, however, need a bowl of cereal. I get Cameron up, and we get our food. I sit on the couch again with my bowl, trying to draw out the morning a bit. Brennon is having none of it though. He is watching me, and as soon as I eat my last bite, he says, "OK, let's start school."

"Alright, alright." I lean over and grab the Bible while Cameron sits in his chair finishing his breakfast. We are reading through Acts, so I turn to where I placed a Post-It to mark my spot. It happens to be the last chapter. I read it, then close the book. Cameron, who is usually my stoic one, decides to tease me a bit. "Mom, what would you do if that snake bit you like it did Paul?" I would have died of a heart attack before the venom could ever have gotten to me, that's what, so I say so.

We pray our usual daily prayer, asking God to *please* help us through this school day: to help us have patience with one another, to cause things to go as smoothly as possible, to help us to learn all that we need to know for our futures. We pray some form of this prayer every day, but I don't think the boys realize that this prayer is serious to me. *Please* help, Lord. This is hard. Please help.

We lift our heads, and I shuffle among the books in my homeschool bag to find our current read aloud, *The Bark of the Bog Owl*. We are all loving this book. As a

87

matter of fact, we are supposed to be reading *Across Five Aprils* for our current curriculum, but the boys really disliked that book. I had just gotten *The Bark of the Bog Owl* from the library last week and had decided to give the kids a break one day and read it instead. This book was so good that I decided to permanently switch to it and stop reading *Across Five Aprils*. Today I am determined that we are only going to read one chapter though because we have other things to do. When the chapter ends, I stop reading and go to close the book.

"Nooooo," says Brennon, "keep going."

"If we have time at the end, we can read another chapter."

I pluck out the history book from the bag next. By this time, both boys have their thinking putty and are smoothing it across their knees or letting it drape down their fingers. Today's lesson is about what happened politically after the Civil War, the decisions that Lincoln made and how his opponents were not happy with those decisions. It ended with Lincoln's assassination. I shut the book and pause for a moment to see if the boys have any comments. Cameron has one: "I would not have been soft on the South like Lincoln was. If I won the war, I would have crushed the Confederates afterward."

Brennon's contributions is, "Harsh, Cameron." This starts a lively debate between Cameron and me about what Lincoln should or should not have done to the South. I'm a nurturer, so of course I agreed with Lincoln that the Confederates should be brought back into the fold and built back up. Our history curriculum provides some comprehension questions, but I skip these. I much prefer discussions like the one we just had, which indicate comprehension.

Once we all settle back down from our debate, laughing at each other because we think so differently, it is time for science. Science is Cameron's least favorite subject, so he groans. Brennon perks up though. Science is fascinating to him; this is why I let him join in on Cameron's seventh grade science curriculum. He is more than capable of keeping up with Cameron in this area. I'm not sure what I'm going to do with Brennon later on because eventually we may run out of sciences. I'll cross that bridge when I come to it.

I read aloud a section about the effect of experimental variables on the experiments, how some are good and how you want to eliminate others. I made copies of the questions last week, so I pull them out of my file folder where I keep all of their weekly sheets. Once they both have one and a pencil, they get to work.

I sit there quietly and watch Brennon happily writing away, enthusiastically answering the questions. I glance over at Cameron and see he is fiercely frowning. It's like I can visibly see the dark storm cloud forming over his head. Uh oh. I try to step in before he completely melts down. I think the problem might be that he has to write by hand instead of type. He has dysgraphia, which makes writing a struggle for him. I try to use a cheerful voice when I offer to help him although my whole body tenses up, remembering the years of battles that Cameron and I have had.

"Cameron, do you want me to write your answers for you? You can just tell me the answer and I will write it?" We will focus on handwriting later in the day, but right now, I am more interested in him learning the science content than I am in him using his handwriting.

"NO, this is stupid." He throws his pencil on the floor. The questions are about an experiment that a student did on potted plants. He had twelve potted plants and gave them each a different amount of fertilizer. He measured the growth after a period of time to see which one grew the most. There was a chart at the top of the question showing the results. The questions ask what I consider to be easy questions about the chart—all you had to do was read the chart and tell what the experimental variables were. I check with Cameron to make sure that he thoroughly understands what an experimental variable was. I truly don't know what has set him off. Because of his Asperger's, sometimes it is hard for him to communicate his thoughts to me.

"Cameron. Why is it stupid? Do you need help answering the questions?"

"No, I can answer the question fine. But it's stupid. I hate plants. I don't care how much fertilizer I have to use to make them grow. I'm never going to own plants."

I sit there staring at him for a moment, processing what he said. Somehow, in Cameron's mind, which is not neurotypical, he thought I was making him learn a fact—how much fertilizer to use on plants. Instead, he was supposed to be learning a skill—how to analyze data. Suddenly, I start laughing. Big belly laughs. His eyes get wide, and he looks at me with a startled expression.

"Why are you laughing?" He starts to half chuckle because he is unsure what is going on.

Still laughing, I explain what he is supposed to be learning—the skill of reading the chart and analyzing data, not the specific fact of how much fertilizer plants need. His face clears up and comprehension dawns. Cameron has a wonderfully analytic mind, and he is so smart, but his Asperger's makes him a concrete thinker. He can memorize facts all day long, but when getting into the world of the abstract, he struggles. This was one of those times when he was so clearly an "Aspie."

"I can't believe you are laughing at me," he grumbles good-naturedly as he now happily finishes answering the questions. He answers them perfectly and quickly, without help, now that his problem with what I was trying to teach him has been cleared up.

"OK, next up writing. Today is easy because we are just brainstorming." I grab the big whiteboard I have and prop it up on a kitchen chair sitting in our living room for this purpose. Next on our writing schedule is an expository essay on kindness. I use the term "essay" loosely, because Cameron has dyspraxia as well as dysgraphia and Asperger's. These two disorders make it difficult for him to organize his thoughts and to write sentences. So all I can get out of him is about a paragraph. Even getting that much is like squeezing blood from a stone. Brennon is the opposite and will ramble on if I don't reign him in. I explain what an expository essay is, and we spend the next fifteen minutes going over the who, what, when, where, why, and how of kindness. I write keywords on the board as the boys answer these questions. I notice most of the ideas are coming from Brennon, so I prompt Cameron a few times directly to get some of his thoughts on the board.

I check the clock to see where we are on time, and we have plenty left. We have a firm end time of noon for school. This is to save everyone's sanity. Right now, it's only 10:30, and we are wrapping up writing.

"Now on to your individual subjects," I announce. I set each child up with their individual work. Cameron is a bit easier because he is able to keep track of where he is in each subject and just pick up where he left off, reading the next chapter or doing the next unit. Today he has health, logic, cursive practice that helps with his

91

dysgraphia, foreign language, a historical novel that he reads independently, and math. He pops his headphones on and turns on his music while he starts his math. Brennon has ADHD though so needs me to show him specifically what to do. I will hand him his subjects one by one to the page that he needs to be on, otherwise he will turn to the wrong section and do that wrong section. (Ask me how I know.) Today his list is the same as Cameron's minus the logic. He also has some copy work to do.

"When you guys are done, let me know and we will do your spelling tests." It is only Wednesday, but both boys have already learned their spelling lists for the week, so there isn't any reason to wait until Friday.

I sit down on the couch and wait for a while to make sure each is settling into his work. After a bit, I pick up *The Elements of Style* by Strunk and White. I'm reviewing it to see if it is something I can use with the boys in our school. I think that it will be a great resource but may be more appropriate for when they get to high school. I flip through the pages and start thinking about how I will integrate it into an English course. I stop occasionally to hand Brennon his next subject. Putting the book aside, I pull out my binder, open it to the school year calendar, and circle today's date. It is only the beginning of October and we are already at day fifty-six. Only 124 days to go.

"Mom," says Cameron, "I'm ready for my spelling quiz." Cameron ends up finishing the school day twenty-five minutes early, so he takes the book he is reading for fun and goes to lie on his bed. Brennon then starts watching the clock. He is a slower reader and worker than Cameron is, so he is usually the last to finish. Sometimes, I will give Cameron a little extra work on the sly, just so Brennon can have a chance to finish first and feel more confident. Brennon finishes the last word of his copy work at 11:59. He hasn't done his spelling test yet, and he knows it.

"I still have to do my spelling test."

"That's okay, we can just do that tomorrow. We'll do it first thing when we start our individual subjects." He happily hops up with a grin and runs off. I collect all the books and papers from the morning and stash them back in the homeschool bag then head to the kitchen to brew another cup of coffee.

How About a Little Fun?

Afterword

Every year I work more toward a simple homeschool. I constantly ask what I can make better, easier, and simpler. There have been a lot of catalysts for change in our home over the years. And simplifying a homeschool is a process that cannot happen overnight.

I know this is a book, and you are here to get ideas. But can we turn it into a game and a conversation?

First, the game. What do you think was the single greatest catalyst for simplifying my homeschool? I wonder if you will be able to guess. I hint at it in the book a few times. If you leave a review for this book on Amazon, at the end of your review, leave me a personal message with the answer to this question. I will read it. No peaking at comments on others' reviews though.

Second, the conversation. Can we have a conversation about creating a simple homeschool? How are *you* doing that? Is there something you are doing that makes your school life simple that I didn't mention here? Please tell me. Tag me on Instagram at @christyrucker. I'd like to implement it myself in our homeschool and share your post with others.

And if you are using any ideas from this book, or even just enjoying it, tag me on Instagram at @christyrucker. I'd love to see what you have going on in your homeschool and share your post with others so we can all stay inspired.

Made in the USA
Middletown, DE
01 September 2020

18011306R00057